SHOENIQUE

12 SUPERCOOL WAYS TO CUSTOMIZE YOUR FOOTWEAR

Tessa Sillars-Powell

WELLFLEET
PRESS

An imprint of Quarto Publishing Group USA Inc.
142 West 36th Street, 4th Floor
New York, New York 10018

WELLFLEET PRESS and the distinctive Wellfleet Press logo are trademarks of Quarto Publishing Group USA Inc.

A Quintet Book
Copyright © 2015 Quintet Publishing Limited

QTT.SHNQ

This book was conceived, designed and produced by:
Quintet Publishing Limited
4th Floor, Sheridan House
114–116 Western Road
Hove, East Sussex
BN3 1DD

Project Editor: Cheryl Brown
Publishing Assistant: Alice Sambrook
Photographer: Simon Pask
Designer: Maria Mokina
Art Director: Michael Charles
Editorial Director: Alana Smythe
Publisher: Mark Searle
The Ombre Sneakers project was designed by Aimee Santos.
All other projects were designed by the author Tessa Sillars-Powell.

ISBN-13: 978-1-57715-110-4

Printed in China by the Hung Hing Printing Group Limited.

2 4 6 8 10 9 7 5 3 1

www.quartous.com

Warning! This kit contains small parts, not intended for use by children younger than 7. Not to be sold separately.

CONTENTS

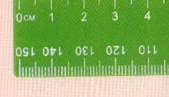

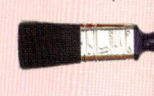

INTRODUCTION

SHOES ARE A VITAL PART OF ANY WARDROBE, NOT LEAST BECAUSE THEY PROVIDE OUR FEET WITH PROTECTION FOR THE 8,000 STEPS WE WALK ON AVERAGE EVERY DAY, BUT THEY CAN ALSO BE WORN TO EXPRESS OUR INDIVIDUAL STYLE. SEEMINGLY THE LEAST VISIBLE PART OF AN OUTFIT, THEY CAN MAKE OR BREAK AN ENSEMBLE—STYLE STARTS FROM THE TOES UP, SO WHAT BETTER WAY TO SHOW OFF YOUR CREATIVE SKILLS THAN BY CUSTOMIZING YOUR OWN ONE-OF-A-KIND CREATIONS?

This book will guide you through 12 fun project tutorials to inspire you to create your own unique shoes, by customizing pairs you might already own or that are easy to buy. The designs fall into four of the most popular footwear styles—flats, sandals, sneakers and boots. But don't worry if your base shoes aren't exactly the same as mine. The ideas can easily be adapted to suit your needs.

FLATS A popular everyday choice due to their comfort—but that doesn't mean they have to lack style. They come in many different varieties, including pretty ballet pumps, sensible brogues and lightweight summer espadrilles. Plain pairs of flats are cheap and easy to find, providing a great base for your customized designs. There's no limit to the creative finishes you can achieve!

SANDALS One of the oldest styles of footwear, there are two bang up-to-date designs for you to try. Both are great examples of how inexpensive flip-flops can provide the perfect base for creating bespoke sandals. The designs are lightweight, use basic tools and can be made to match an existing outfit. So get ready for the sun with simple customizations that can be easily adapted to suit your personal style.

SNEAKERS Not only popular on the sports field, sneakers are the footwear of choice for those looking to combine casual comfort with cutting-edge fashion on the street. Basic, plain versions aren't difficult to come by, and you can use them as a launch pad for your creative design. Sneakers are made in a range of materials from natural canvas, perfect for dyeing, to synthetic plastics and polyesters, better suited for gluing embellishments onto.

BOOTS Ideal for those colder days, this sturdier style of footwear offers your feet maximum protection. The downside is that such practical choices often come in quite plain colors and styles. You can use a variety of materials from metal studs to DIY duct tape stickers to brighten up your boots, although as they are generally made from thicker and more durable materials, customizing them will involve a little more ingenuity.

Before choosing your perfect pair, take a little time to get to grips with the tools and equipment you might need and the embellishing materials you will want, then get ready to hit your stride and become a "shoenique" designer.

TOOLS & EQUIPMENT

WHEN CUSTOMIZING SHOES, THERE ARE A FEW REALLY USEFUL EVERYDAY CRAFT TOOLS AND EQUIPMENT THAT CAN HELP YOU TO ACHIEVE YOUR DESIRED EFFECTS. THIS BASIC SELECTION IS A GOOD STARTING POINT, ALTHOUGH THE "YOU WILL NEED" LISTS FOR EACH PROJECT WILL ITEMIZE ALL YOUR REQUIREMENTS. ALWAYS MAKE SURE THAT YOU USE THE RIGHT TOOL FOR THE JOB TO KEEP CRAFTING SAFELY.

Ruler and tape measure: essential for symmetrical designs and evenly spaced embellishments.

Scissors: keep several pairs—one exclusively for cutting paper and craft materials, a fabric-cutting pair and a stronger pair for tougher materials, like thick PVC.

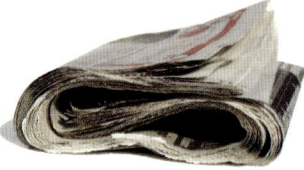

Newspaper: handy to protect your work surfaces and for masking off areas on your shoes that you don't want to color when painting.

Masking tape: 2"-wide is used, but a standard $^{3}/_{4}$"-wide roll is also useful to have.

All-purpose glue: for fixing lightweight embellishments in place; for heavier embellishments, use contact adhesive.

Wax paper: to make the backing for DIY duct tape stickers.

Tracing paper: for making embroidery pattern templates.

Fine sandpaper: for preparing plastic surfaces for painting.

Cardboard: this has many uses—making stencils and glue spreading to name just two.

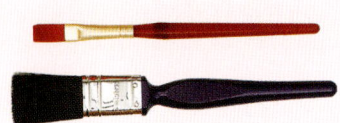

Paintbrushes: keep a range of widths—use narrow ones to apply detail accents and wider ones to paint larger areas more quickly.

Petroleum jelly: rub onto rubber soles to protect from dye; brush into leather to buff it up.

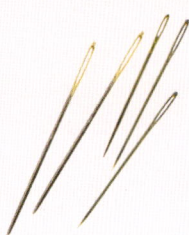

Embroidery and sewing needles: in a variety of sizes to suit different thicknesses of shoe material.

Mod Podge: a multi-purpose, water-based sealer glue; used to stick glitter embellishments onto shoes for a water-resistant finish.

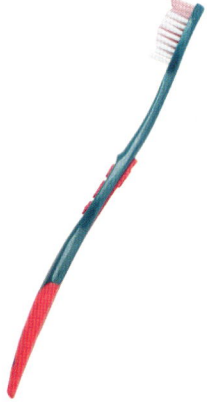

Toothbrush: to clean up shoes pre-customization; also used to apply paints, dyes and glues.

Craft knife: useful for cutting most materials; choose one with a sturdy handle and retractable blade, and always use with care.

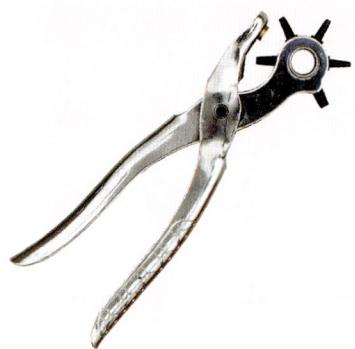

Hole punch pliers: to make neat holes in leather and suede; usually revolves for holes of varying sizes.

Glue gun: ideal for attaching larger embellishments to your shoes, but use with care as the glue can get very hot!

EMBELLISHING MATERIALS

YOU CAN USE SO MANY EXCITING MATERIALS TO CUSTOMIZE YOUR FOOTWEAR—YOUR CHOICE CAN DEPEND ON THE TYPE OF SHOE YOU ARE WORKING ON, WHETHER MADE FROM SYNTHETIC PLASTIC OR NATURAL CANVAS. YOU ARE ENCOURAGED TO EXPERIMENT, BUT JUST BE AWARE THAT DIFFERENT MATERIALS CAN HAVE DIFFERENT EFFECTS WHEN THEY COME INTO CONTACT WITH CERTAIN ADHESIVES, SO IT IS IMPORTANT TO ALWAYS READ THE PRODUCT MANUFACTURER'S INSTRUCTIONS.

Duct tape: for DIY stickers; choose a quality water-resistant brand.

Craft foam: can be easily cut into fun shapes with craft scissors.

Spray paint: instant color update; always use in a well-ventilated area.

Permanent marker pens: for creating patterns and outlining embellishments.

Embroidery floss: thick, colorful floss for embroidering decorative details onto soft fabric shoes.

Nail polish: for achieving a detailed gloss effect on a small area; strong finish in exciting colors and effects.

Glitter: use fine-fleck glitter for a smooth finish, less likely to chip.

Beads: choose beads with holes large enough to be threaded.

Buttons: best attached with contact adhesive or hot glue, or sewn on.

Ribbon: available in lots of widths and colors for cute bows.

Yarn: for making pom-poms—acrylic blends are most durable.

Felt: use quality, dense felt approx. ⅛" thick for long-lasting creations.

QUICK CUSTOMIZING TIPS

THE PROJECTS FEATURED IN THIS BOOK ARE QUICK TO MAKE, BUT WHEN TIME IS AGAINST YOU, HERE ARE A FEW SIMPLE AND SUPER-FAST WAYS TO INSTANTLY CHANGE THE LOOK OF A TIRED PAIR OF SHOES.

⊕ CHANGE YOUR SHOELACES Give your shoes an instant makeover with some of the many different types of lace out there. There are so many to choose from—straight or curly, thick or thin, glittery, patterned or crazy colored, and glow-in-the-dark ones too.

⊕ SWAP SHOESTRINGS FOR RIBBON TIES For immediate elegance, use a pretty, quality ribbon to lace up your shoes, but be sure to fix the end of the ribbon to prevent it from fraying.

⊕ DITCH A DULL BUCKLE There are so many beautiful buckles made, why be content with a plain fastening? Either paint your existing ones, adorn them with craft gems and crystals, or choose glitzy store-bought versions.

⊕ BUCKLE UP FOR FUN Who said a buckle had to function as a fastening? Make a false strap from a scrap of leftover leather, thread it through a customized buckle, and stitch or glue in place.

⊕ ZIPPER IT UP Use colorful zippers as a decorative feature to embellish shoes and boots—just stick on using contact adhesive or hot glue.

⊕ MAKE SHOE CHARMS AND MIX THEM UP Use hook-and-loop tape to create interchangeable charms for a pair of sneakers. Available in lots of different colors and sizes, the tape comes in two parts: a piece with tiny hooks on it, and a piece with tiny loops.

ANATOMY OF A SHOE

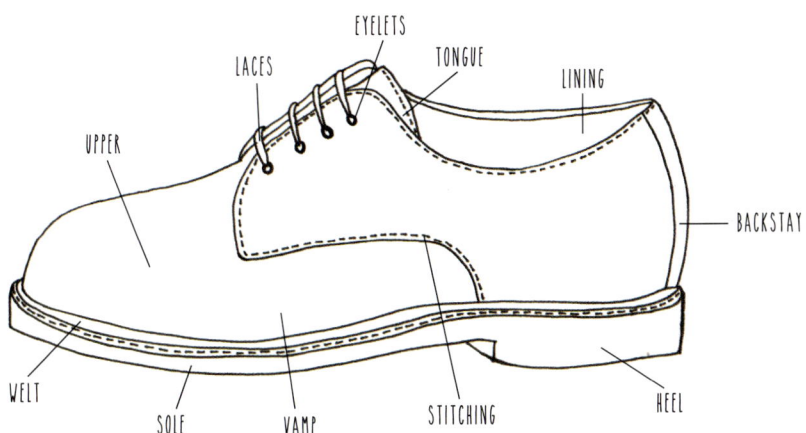

EYELETS

LACES

TONGUE

LINING

UPPER

BACKSTAY

WELT

SOLE

VAMP

STITCHING

HEEL

CUTE AS A BUTTON

THESE SWEET AND SIMPLE FLATS ARE FUN AND EASY TO MAKE. ADDING EMBELLISHMENTS LIKE BUTTONS AND RIBBON BOWS IS A GREAT WAY OF BRINGING CHARACTER TO A CLASSIC SHOE STYLE. CHOOSE FLATS WITH A ROUND OR A POINTED TOE, BUT JUST MAKE SURE THERE IS A BIG ENOUGH SURFACE AREA TO STICK YOUR BUTTONS ONTO.

YOU WILL NEED

- O *1 pair of flats*
- O *Approx. 30 buttons ranging in size from ¼" to 1" diameter*
- O *Narrow ribbon, 24" long*
- O *All-purpose glue*
- O *Hole punch pliers*
- O *Pencil*

Instant fashion fun!

1 Mark lightly in pencil where you would like the buttons to be positioned on one of the shoes—you will be using half the buttons on each shoe. Mirror these markings onto the other shoe, so they are symmetrical.

2 Divide your buttons into two matching piles. Turn the buttons upside down and spread a thin layer of all-purpose glue onto each—don't let any drip through the buttonholes. Place the buttons, one at a time, in the marked positions on each shoe, and supporting from the inside, press down firmly to stick securely in place.

3 Use the hole punch pliers to pierce a ⅛" hole through the backstay of each shoe, approx. ⅜" from the top.

4 Cut your ribbon in half and thread a length through each hole. Tie each ribbon in a neat bow to complete.

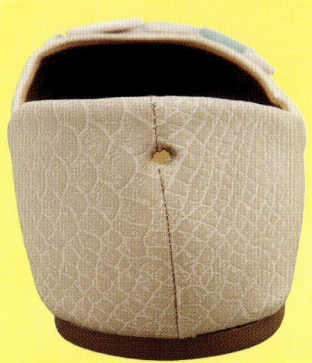

 **TIP**

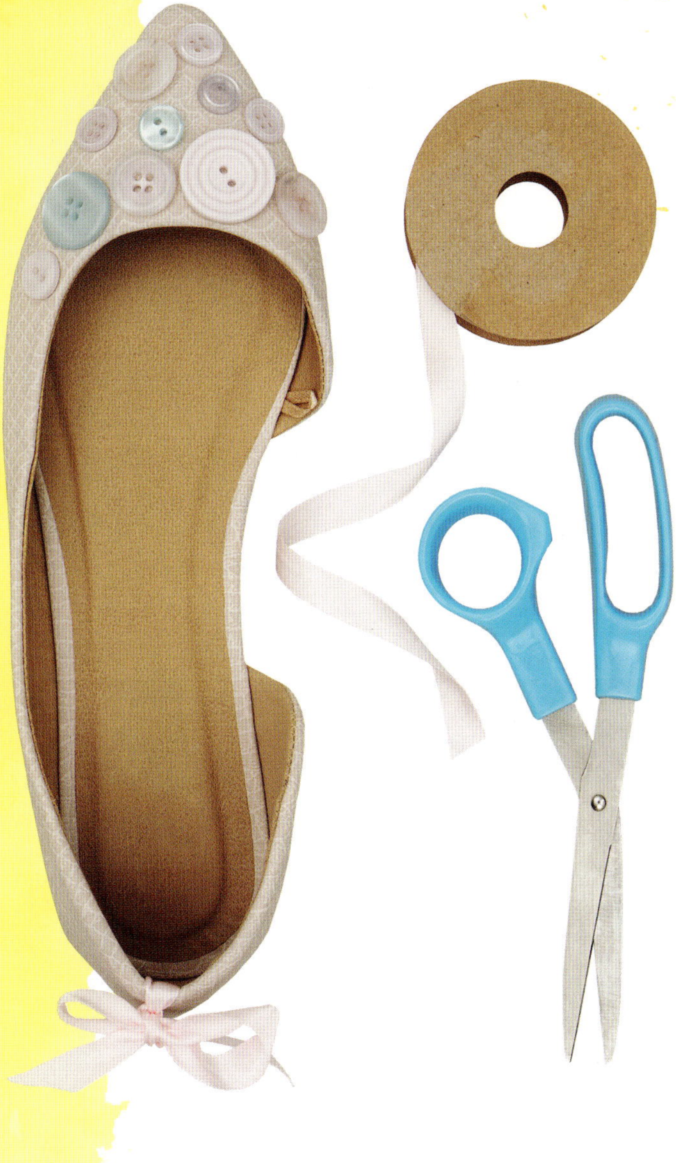

To ensure your buttons stay stuck, the whole surface of the button must be in contact with the shoe—use smaller buttons on curved areas to achieve this.

FOX FOOTED

RELEASE YOUR INNER ANIMAL WITH THESE ADORABLE FOX-THEMED FLATS. USING STENCILING, SIMPLE FELT DECORATION AND DIY POM-POMS, THIS PROJECT HAS LOTS OF NEW SKILLS FOR YOU TO TRY OUT, AND THE DESIGN CAN BE EASILY ADAPTED TO MAKE OTHER ANIMALS. WE HAVE CHOSEN A PAIR OF ORANGE FLATS, BUT LIGHT BROWN ONES WOULD WORK JUST AS WELL WITH BROWN FELT AND YARN EMBELLISHMENTS.

YOU WILL NEED

- ♥ *1 pair of orange flats*
- ♥ *White spray paint*
- ♥ *Orange felt, 4" × 2"*
- ♥ *Black felt, 8" × 2"*
- ♥ *Orange yarn*
- ♥ *Wax paper, 16" × 8"*
- ♥ *Double-sided carpet tape*

- ♥ *2"-wide masking tape*
- ♥ *Pencil, pen and ruler*
- ♥ *All-purpose glue*
- ♥ *Scissors*
- ♥ *Fork*
- ♥ *Hole punch pliers*

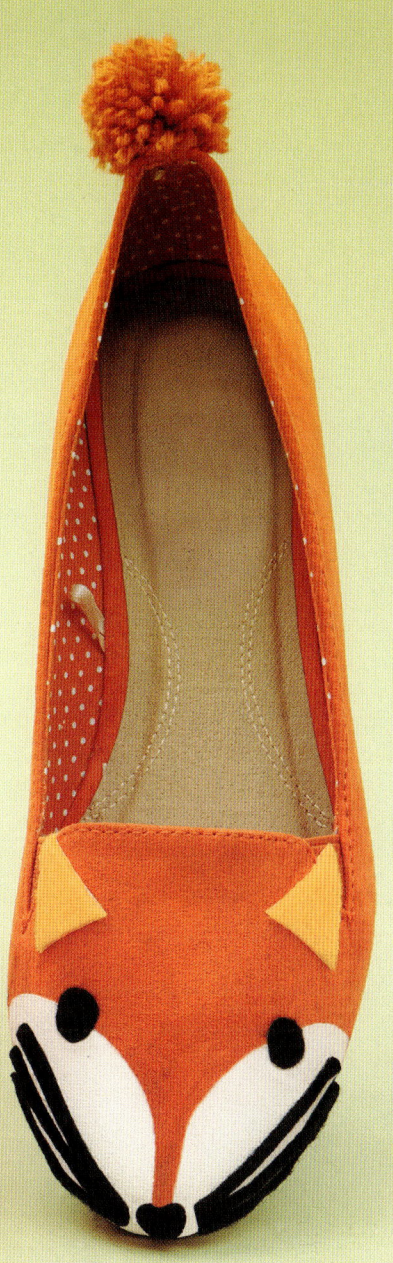

1 Fold the wax paper in half and cut into two, these pieces will form one stencil for each shoe. Take the first piece and stick a length of masking tape close to its bottom edge. Cut another length of tape and stick it down to overlap the edge of the first piece by ¼". Repeat twice more.

2 Starting on the line where the first two strips of masking tape overlap, use a pencil and the inside of the masking tape roll to draw two semi-circles about ¼" apart, then go over the lines with a pen to make them stand out (see photo). Now take your ruler and continue their line straight down to create two arch shapes.

3 Trim the edge of the taped area to the straight line of the outer edges of the arch shapes, and cut out the arch shapes to give you your stencil. Peel the masking tape stencil from the wax paper and stick it centrally onto one of the shoes. Make a second stencil and attach it onto the other shoe.

4 Working in a well-ventilated area (outdoors if possible), carefully spray the toe of each shoe with white spray paint. (You may want to cover the backs of the shoes with newspaper to keep them spray paint free.) Once the paint is completely dry, remove the masking tape stencils.

5 Stick double-sided carpet tape onto both pieces of felt. On the tape side of the black felt, use a pencil to draw two small heart shapes for noses, four circles for eyes and 12 thin, long strips for whiskers. On the tape side of the orange felt, draw four triangles for ears.

6 Cut out your drawn shapes from the tape-backed felt pieces. One by one, peel the backing paper off each shape and stick them onto the shoes to create the foxes faces.

7 Use the hole punch pliers to pierce a ⅛" hole through the backstay of each shoe, ⅜" from the top. To make the foxes tails, make two pom-poms from orange yarn. Start by wrapping the yarn around the prongs of a fork until you have an oval shape when viewed side on.

8 Thread an 8" length of yarn between the prongs of the fork and tie it tightly around the yarn bundle (**do not trim**). Slide the bundle off the fork and carefully cut each looped end to create a pom-pom. To fix each pom-pom tail onto the shoes, thread one of the untrimmed yarn ends through each hole and tie securely.

TIP

Choose thick well-matted felt pieces as these will hold together better when cutting the small detail pieces for the foxes faces.

GLITTER BROGUES

ADD A SPARKLE TO YOUR STEP BY CREATING YOUR VERY OWN PAIR OF RAZZLE-DAZZLE BROGUES—THERE'LL NEVER BE A DULL DAY WITH THESE IN YOUR WARDROBE. GOLD COMPLEMENTS ANY SHADE OF SHOE, BUT WITH GLITTER AVAILABLE IN SO MANY DIFFERENT COLORS, YOU CAN HAVE FUN CHOOSING YOUR FAVORITE. THIS PROJECT FOCUSES ON PAINTING SKILLS THAT REQUIRE A STEADY HAND.

YOU WILL NEED

- ★ *1 pair of brogues*
- ★ *Gold glitter*
- ★ *Pale pink nail polish*
- ★ *Mod Podge*
- ★ *Chalk*
- ★ *Bowl*
- ★ *Spoon*
- ★ *Paintbrush*
- ★ *Cocktail stick*

Ready to shine?

1 Remove the laces and use chalk to mark out the areas where you want the glitter to be painted on each shoe—we chose to apply glitter to follow the lines of stitching on the upper and backstay, and to cover the tongue of each shoe.

2 In a bowl, mix even quantities of Mod Podge and glitter to make a smooth paste, using a spoon to break down any lumps. Carefully paint the glitter mixture onto the marked areas on each shoe, going right up to but not over any lines of stitching. Once dry, paint a second coat if required.

3 Use pale pink nail polish to highlight areas on the upper and backstay of each shoe, painting your lines as neatly as you can.

4 Using a cocktail stick, add small dots of the remaining glitter mixture to fill all the holes on the toes of each shoe for extra twinkle. Leave the shoes to dry, then re-lace.

TIP

Use a damp cloth and an old toothbrush to remove any unwanted glitter from each shoe before it fully dries.

EMBROIDERED ESPADRILLES

THE SOFT FABRIC UPPER OF A PAIR OF ESPADRILLES IS THE PERFECT BLANK CANVAS FOR ADDING DECORATIVE DETAILING WITH A FEW SIMPLE EMBROIDERY STITCHES. DRAW YOUR DESIGN ONTO TRACING PAPER, MAKE A COPY, PIN IT IN PLACE AND STITCH THROUGH—A SIMPLE YET EFFECTIVE METHOD FOR ACHIEVING PERFECT SYMMETRY. THERE'S NO LIMIT TO THE PATTERNS YOU CAN ADD, BUT A SIMPLE STARBURST IS GREAT FOR A FIRST ATTEMPT.

YOU WILL NEED

- *1 pair of plain espadrilles*
- *Embroidery floss in 3 contrasting colors*
- *Tracing paper*
- *Pencil*
- *Ruler*
- *Scissors*
- *Embroidery needle*
- *Pins*

1, 2, 3, sew!

1 Place one of the espadrilles onto a piece of tracing paper and use a pencil to draw around the toe of the shoe, finishing in line with where the upper stops at the front.

2 Draw a pattern onto the traced outline of the toe of the shoe, but not too close to the edge. Turn over your tracing and go over the lines to make a copy onto a second piece of tracing paper for the other shoe. Trim each template so that there is a border roughly 2" from the edge of the shoe outline.

3 Pin the templates to the uppers. Thread the needle with your first embroidery floss color and tie a knot at the end. Working on one shoe at a time, bring the needle out through the back of the upper at the center of your pattern. Work long stitches back into the center following your pencil lines; to finish, run the needle through a few stitches on the reverse and trim the excess floss.

4 Repeat to stitch the smaller starburst in the same way, using another floss color, then work the circles in a third color. The tracing paper will start to crack as you embroider; when you have finished, remove the pins, and carefully tear the tracing paper out of the stitches to reveal your design.

TIP

A curved needle will help if you are finding it difficult to reach inside the toe of your shoe.

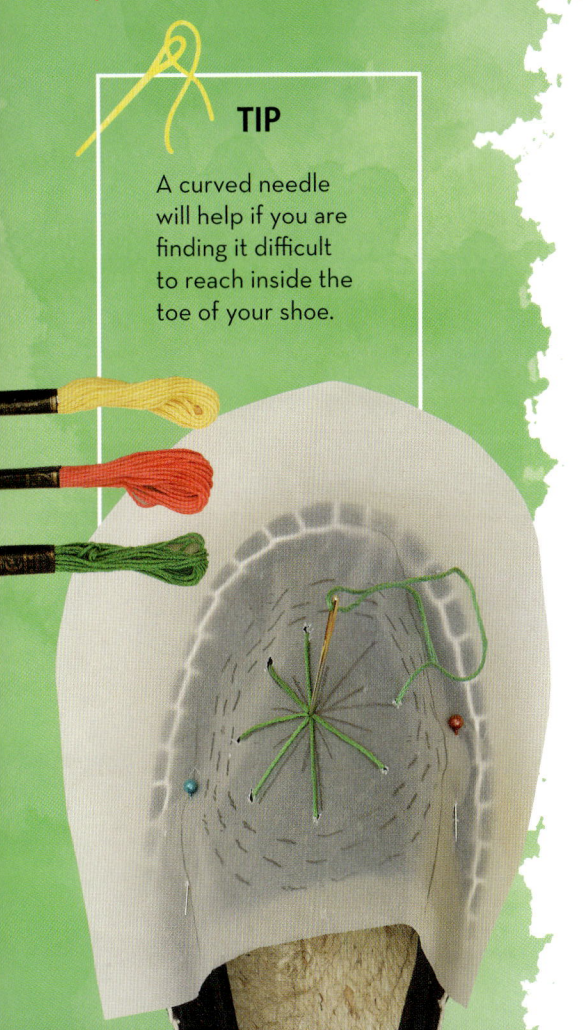

BEADED FLIP-FLOPS

TRANSFORMED FROM BEACH TRIP STANDARD TO WEDDING PARTY STUNNER, THESE ELEGANT FLIP-FLOPS ARE STYLISH ENOUGH TO WEAR WHATEVER THE OCCASION. FLIP-FLOP BASES CAN BE SOURCED RELATIVELY CHEAPLY, BUT BY FINISHING THEM OFF YOURSELF YOU CAN CREATE BESPOKE FOOTWEAR. SO THRIFTY YET SO SIMPLE—JUST WRAP WITH RIBBON AND USE AS A BASE TO SEW ON CLUSTERS OF BEADS TO MATCH AN OUTFIT, OR YOUR FAVORITE JEWELRY.

YOU WILL NEED

- *1 pair of plain flip-flops*
- *⅝"-wide white ribbon, 120" long*
- *Approx. 30 mixed beads in white, pearl and metal*
- *White sewing thread*
- *Scissors*
- *Sewing needle*

It's a bling thing!

1 Cut your ribbon into four lengths: two measuring 40" and two measuring 20". Take a 40" length and tie it at its mid point to the base of the post at the front of the flip-flop.

2 Wrap both strands of the ribbon around the post until the strap forks, then separate the ribbon strands and continue to wrap them around each of the straps. At the end of the straps, secure the ribbon with a few stitches (see detail photo) and trim any excess.

3 Take a 20" length of ribbon, loop it over the fork in the strap and secure it with a few stitches (see detail photo). Weave the ribbon over and under the two straps from side to side, filling in the V-shape inbetween to create a neat woven plait covering about 3 ½" of each strap. Sew the ribbon to itself and trim the excess.

4 You now have a base to sew your beads onto. Thread a needle and sew your first bead in place. Continue to cover the V-shaped ribbon section with beads, mixing up bead size and type to create a cluster effect. Repeat to make your second flip-flop.

TIP

For extra sparkle, sew more beads along the top edges of the straps.

BRAIDED SANDALS

TO TRANSFORM A PAIR OF TOE-RUBBING FLIP-FLOPS INTO SUPER-COMFORTABLE SUMMER SANDALS, ALL YOU NEED IS A PAIR OF SCISSORS AND A LIGHTWEIGHT SCARF. THE PLASTIC STRAPS OF THE FLIP-FLOPS ARE CUT AWAY AND REPLACED WITH EASY-WEAR PLAITED FABRIC STRAPS THAT ARE TIED AROUND THE ANKLE FOR A LAID-BACK BEACH LOOK. BRAIDING IS SO SIMPLE TO DO WHATEVER YOUR SKILL LEVEL.

YOU WILL NEED

➤ *1 pair of plain flip-flops*

➤ *1 long, lightweight fabric scarf*

➤ *Scissors*

➤ *Pencil*

Unleash your beach goddess

1 Cut your scarf lengthways into six strands. Split these into two groups of three strands, and tie a knot at the center point of each to give you six distinct strands on each fabric pile.

2 Cut off the straps from one of your flip-flops (see detail photo). Take one of the fabric piles and thread each of the fabric strands through the central hole at the front of the flip-flop sole, from the underside to the top. Make sure that the knot stays on the base of the sole—it may help to use the unsharpened end of a pencil to push the fabric through. You should have six fabric strands coming out of the hole.

3 Start to plait three of the strands together, continuing until you have created a length long enough to reach the side hole, with enough slack to fit across the top of your foot. Thread the ends of the plaited strands down through the side hole to the underside, as shown in the photo below. Tie a knot, and then thread the strands back up through the hole, using a pencil as in Step 2.

4 Making sure that the knot stays on the underside of the sole, continue to plait the strands (as seen on the left-hand side of the photo below). Continue to the end of the strap on each side, then tie the strands securely in a knot (see right-hand side of the photo below). Trim the strand ends to the same length if necessary. Repeat Steps 2–4 to make the second sandal.

TIP

For longer straps to tie higher up your leg gladiator-style, use one scarf per flip-flop.

OMBRE SNEAKERS

PLAIN WHITE SNEAKERS ARE A GREAT STARTING POINT FOR SHOE DIY-ERS. THIS OMBRE TUTORIAL USES A DYE PAINT TECHNIQUE TO CREATE A GRADUATED TINT EFFECT WITH JUST TWO COLORS OF FABRIC SPRAY PAINT. THIS METHOD CAN BE USED ACROSS A RANGE OF FABRICS, INCLUDING CANVAS AND COTTON, AND VARIOUS SHOE TYPES. WHY NOT TRY IT OUT ON A PAIR OF PUMPS?

YOU WILL NEED

- *1 pair of plain white canvas sneakers*
- *Fabric spray paint in 2 colors*
- *Petroleum jelly*
- *2 sponge brushes*
- *Toothbrush*
- *Bowl*

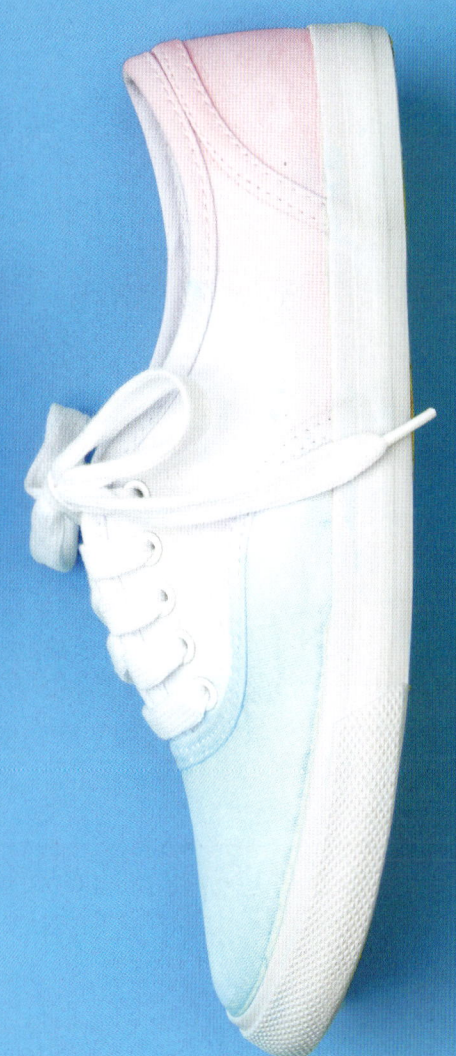

Get set to go girl

1 Remove the shoelaces. Rub petroleum jelly along the rubber sole and welt of the sneakers. Doing so will prevent this area from being painted. Fill the bowl with water and use one of the sponge brushes to dab water onto the fabric part of the sneaker until it is entirely damp.

2 Spray the front tip of your sneaker with your first color of fabric spray paint, and quickly spread the paint toward the center of the sneaker using the wet sponge brush. Continue brushing water onto the spray-painted area to create an ombre look.

3 Spray the back of the sneaker with your second color of fabric spray paint. Quickly spread the paint toward the center of the sneaker using the second wet sponge brush. Continue this to create an ombre look.

4 Using a toothbrush, scrub the sole and welt under running water until the petroleum jelly is completely removed. Repeat the entire process on the second sneaker. Let the sneakers dry overnight before re-lacing.

TIP

Rub the soles of the sneakers with baking soda; it will absorb the petroleum jelly and rub straight off.

CHEVRON SNEAKERS

REVEAL YOUR HIDDEN ARTIST WITH THIS STYLISH PAIR OF SPORTY SNEAKERS, DESIGNED TO ENSURE YOU STAND OUT FROM THE CROWD BOTH ON AND OFF THE PITCH. THE CLASSIC CHEVRON DESIGN IS DRAWN WITH COLORFAST PENS. THERE ARE LOTS OF DIFFERENT FABRIC MARKERS AVAILABLE IN DIFFERENT THICKNESSES AND COLORS, AND THE ONLY SKILL YOU'LL NEED IS A STEADY HAND.

YOU WILL NEED

- ✔ *1 pair of plain white sneakers*
- ✔ *2 fabric markers*
- ✔ *1 piece of card, approx. 8" × 6"*
- ✔ *Masking tape*
- ✔ *Pencil*
- ✔ *Ruler*
- ✔ *Scissors*

1 Use a pencil and ruler to draw a neat zigzag line down the length of the piece of card, then use scissors to carefully cut along the drawn zigzag line to make your chevron stencil.

2 Remove the shoelaces. Starting at the toe, bend your stencil around one of the sneakers and stick it to the sole with masking tape.

3 Take your first color of fabric marker and draw your first zigzag line. Unpeel the stencil and reposition it a little way back; draw another zigzag line with your second fabric marker, leaving a white space inbetween each chevron. Continue to work from toe to heel, drawing lines in alternate colors.

4 When you get to the back of the sneaker, draw the chevrons so that they are perpendicular to the welt. Then return to the tongue of the sneaker to extend the chevron lines under the upper flaps across the whole width. Repeat Steps 2–4 to make your second sneaker and re-lace the sneakers to finish.

TIP

Get creative with your color choices—draw chevrons in the seven colors of the rainbow.

WINGED SNEAKERS

YOU'LL BE FLYING HIGH FROM ALL THE COMPLIMENTS YOU'LL RECEIVE FROM THIS QUICK-FIX CUSTOMIZATION. GET CREATIVE WITH YOUR WING SHAPES: OURS ARE MADE FROM KITCHEN SPONGE CLOTHS, ALTHOUGH CRAFT FOAM ALSO WORKS WELL—BOTH ARE REALLY DURABLE AND CAN BE EASILY CUT INTO INTRICATE DESIGNS. YOU'LL NEED A STEADY HAND TO DRAW DETAILED LINES AND CUT NEAT SHAPES—THEN SIMPLY LAYER UP AND STICK.

YOU WILL NEED

- *1 pair of high-top sneakers*
- *4 thin kitchen sponge cloths, each 8" × 7"*
- *Acrylic paint, gold or bronze*
- *Medium paintbrush*
- *Fine marker pen*
- *2 pieces of card*
- *All-purpose glue*
- *Pencil*
- *Scissors*
- *Ruler*
- *Tracing paper*

Flying high

1 Using tracing paper and a pencil, trace off the wing templates from page 64. Transfer the templates onto card using the marker pen and cut out to give you your wing patterns. Use the patterns to draw four sets of wings onto the kitchen sponge cloths, and then cut out, making sure to cut inbetween the feather markings too.

2 Paint one side and the edges of all the sponge wings with your acrylic gold or bronze paint, and allow to dry. Turn the wings over, paint the other side and leave to dry once more.

3 Once dry, use plenty of all-purpose glue to stick each set of wings together, so that a medium and a small wing are layered on top of a large wing. You should have four sets of layered wings. Let the glue dry completely before continuing.

4 Spread a line of glue ⅜"-wide on the reverse side of the layered wings taking care to avoid the cut feathers. Position the wings in place at either side of each of the sneakers and leave to dry completely.

TIP

Craft foam comes in an array of colors, so save on painting time by cutting out your wings from a pre-colored sheet.

STUDDED BOOTS

A STURDY PAIR OF BOOTS WILL KEEP YOUR FEET WARM, DRY AND WELL-PROTECTED, BUT WHO SAID YOU HAD TO SETTLE FOR A SOMBER BLACK? BRING A GLINT AND A SHINE TO "SENSIBLE" FOOTWEAR WITH THIS EYE-CATCHING DECORATIVE DESIGN CREATED WITH SQUARE AND ROUND METAL STUDS. STUDS ARE EASY TO FIND, BUT FITTING THEM CAN SOMETIMES REQUIRE A BIT OF FORCE, SO MUSCLE UP—IT'LL BE WORTH IT.

YOU WILL NEED

- ✖ *1 pair of ankle boots*
- ✖ *Square metal studs (with prongs)*
- ✖ *Round metal studs (with prongs)*
- ✖ *Prong press tool*
- ✖ *Pliers*
- ✖ *Chalk marker pen*
- ✖ *Ruler*

Stand out
in a crowd!

1 First undo any straps or laces that might get in your way, then use a chalk marker pen to mark the positions of the square studs—this will vary depending on the design of your boot. Use a ruler to ensure your marks are evenly spaced.

2 Starting at the bottom of your design, carefully push a square stud through so that the prongs come out on the inside of the boot, cautiously feeling with your fingers to check they have gone all the way through.

SAFETY NOTE

The prongs on the studs can be very sharp so be careful when fitting them into position to avoid catching your fingers, especially when pushing down the prongs. Make sure the prongs are pressed smoothly in place as any raised edges can cause damage to socks and abrasions to skin.

3 Use the prong press tool to bend down the prongs on the inside of the boot so that they are securely fixed in place. The prongs should lie completely smooth, as we have demonstrated on a scrap of leather in the detail photo below right—this can be a little difficult as you are working blind on the inside of your boot. If you lay the boot flat on its side, you may find it easier to rub the prong press tool over the prongs.

4 Carefully repeat Steps 2 and 3 to fix the remaining square studs in place on your marked positions. Then take your round studs and use them to fill in any gaps in the pattern, pushing the prongs down as you go. Repeat the entire process to make the second boot.

TIP

If you don't have a prong press tool, a flat-head screwdriver does the job.

RAINY DAY BOOTS

THIS PAIR OF BRIGHTLY DECORATED GUM BOOTS WILL BRING A SMILE TO THE GRAYEST OF DAYS, AND HAVE YOU SPLASHING IN PUDDLES WITH JOY. SPRAY PAINT YOUR BOOTS, THEN GET BUSY ADDING THE CLOUD CUFF AND COLORFUL RAINDROP DESIGN, ALL CUT FROM COLORED DUCT TAPE. IF YOU ARE ABLE TO FIND GUM BOOTS THAT ARE ALREADY THE DESIRED COLOR, YOU CAN SKIP THE FIRST STEP.

YOU WILL NEED

- *1 pair of gum boots*
- *White spray paint (optional)*
- *Blue spray paint*
- *2"-wide duct tape: white, red, green, yellow*
- *Wax paper*
- *Newspaper*
- *Fine sandpaper*
- *Scissors*
- *Black permanent marker pen*

Splish, splash, splosh!

1 Make sure your boots are clean and dry. Cover your work surface with newspaper, and give the boots a light sanding using fine sandpaper before spray painting blue.

TIP

If you have a dark or patterned pair of gum boots, it is a good idea to give them a coat of white spray paint before applying the color to achieve a brighter finish.

2 Stick four or five strips of white duct tape to a length of wax paper, leaving a small gap inbetween each one, and then turn the paper over so that the duct tape is on the underside. Draw clouds along the paper backing of the duct tape lengths using a marker pen.

3 Cut the cloud shapes out—exactly how many you will need will depend on the width of your gum boot, but allow approx. 8-10 for each boot. One by one, peel the cloud stickers off the wax paper, and apply them around the top of each boot about 2" from the edge, overlapping them slightly.

4 Now make the raindrop stickers. Stick a strip of red, green and yellow duct tape to another length of wax paper, remembering to leave a small gap inbetween each strip. Turn the wax paper over so that the duct tape is on the underside.

5 Draw raindrop shapes along the paper backing of the duct tape strips—a few of each color for each boot. Cut the shapes out and divide them into two piles, one for each boot. One by one, peel the raindrop stickers off the wax paper, and apply them to the boots, avoiding the foot areas.

6 Use scissors to trim the top of the boots to the top edge of the clouds to give you a decorative and fun border.

7 Take the black permanent marker pen and outline the raindrops and clouds to make them stand out.

TIP

Be sure to use a good-quality rubberized spray paint, available from your local hardware store or online.

WOOLY WARMERS

THESE COZY BOOTS WILL ENSURE YOU LOOK COOL WHILE KEEPING WARM. BY RECYCLING THE SLEEVES FROM AN OLD SWEATER, AND ADDING SOME RIBBON AND A COUPLE OF BUTTONS TO COMPLEMENT, YOU CAN CREATE AN EFFORTLESS LOOK FOR YOUR BOOTS THAT BEATS ANY STORE-BOUGHT PAIR. FOR THIS PROJECT YOU'LL USE SOME SIMPLE SEWING SKILLS, AND THE ADDITION OF GLUE ENSURES THESE BOOTS ARE DURABLE THROUGH ALL WEATHERS.

YOU WILL NEED

- ✂ *1 pair of soft ankle boots*
- ✂ *Patterned sweater*
- ✂ *⅝"-wide ribbon, approx. 12" long*
- ✂ *2 buttons, ¾" diameter*
- ✂ *All-purpose glue*
- ✂ *Sewing thread and sewing needle*
- ✂ *Scissors*
- ✂ *Tape measure or ruler*

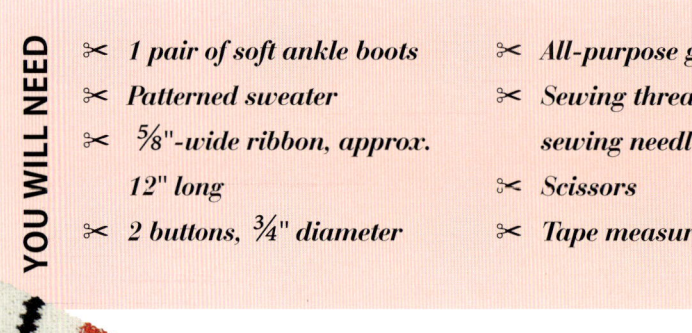

1 Measure 10" from the cuffs of your sweater's sleeves and cut, following the pattern, to give you two tubes of sleeve fabric each measuring 10" long.

2 Turn the sleeve tubes inside out and stretch them over the collar of each boot, so that the cuffs are at the top. Roll them down to expose the tops of the boots.

3 Spread an even 1 ⅛"-wide line of glue along the top edge of each boot. (If your boots have a tongue and laces like ours have, do not glue this area otherwise you won't be able to get them on and off.) Pull up each of the cuffs and stick them to the glue lines; leave the boots to dry.

4 Fold up the cut end of the sleeve tube on one of the boots, turn under its raw edge, and stitch it to the stuck-down cuff so that the edges align neatly, gathering as you go. If your boot has a tongue, fold both the raw edges in at this section, and continue to stitch together. Cut the ribbon into two. Take one piece and stitch it centrally to the inside edge on the outer facing side.

5 Stretch the ribbon over the top of the sleeve tube, and stitch it in place along the bottom (folded) edge on the outside of the outer facing side of the boot, and then stitch the button on top to hide your stitches.

6 Repeat Steps 4 and 5 to sew the remaining length of ribbon and button in place to the outside edge of your second boot.

TIP

Upcycle your remaining sweater off-cuts by making a hat or bag to match your boots.

ABOUT THE AUTHOR

Tessa Sillars-Powell is a professional crafter and writer living in London. She spends her time working on a variety of creative commissions, from making props and costumes to upcycling furniture and customizing clothes. Her hands are always busy creating new ideas and projects, which she loves to share. She has written a number of best-selling instructional craft books and magazines, and presented tutorials for children's television and online channels.

With a background and training in theater craft, Tessa has many practical skills, including woodwork, costume construction and scenic painting. She brings theatrical elements into her designs and always enjoys combining these skills on projects. She has been making things for as long as she can remember and is delighted to have been able to turn her passion into a career.

TEMPLATES

Winged Sneakers
Measure the height of your sneaker from the welt to the collar, and the width from the front of the high-top to the backstay: the large wing shape should measure approximately the same height and about 1" wider, and if it does not, you may need to enlarge or reduce the templates slightly.